Once Upon A Time in Oklahoma

Yvonne Carpenter

MONGREL EMPIRE PRESS
NORMAN, OKLAHOMA, UNITED STATES OF AMERICA

2020

FIRST EDITION, 2020

Once Upon a Time in Oklahoma
© 2020 by Yvonne Carpenter

ISBN 978-1-7323935-7-8

Cover Art
© 2020 by Riley Cabaniss

Author Photo
@2020 by GeoReta Jones

Mongrel Empire Press
Norman, OK

Online catalogue: www.mongrelempire.org

This publisher is a proud member of

COUNCIL OF LITERARY MAGAZINES & PRESSES
w w w . c l m p . o r g

Contents

Acknowledgements

Hours from Harvest, Morning Chores with Snow, Rescue, During the Crash (In the Financial Crisis), *Ain't Nobody that Can Sing Like Me.*

Something About Fire, *Concho River Review*

Spring Calving, *Dos Gatos Press*

March and Inspire Me, *Dragon Poet Review*

Okies Then and Now, *Elegant Rage*

White October, *Grain*

Chipped Marble, *Red Earth Review*

October at the Cattle Auction, Faded Tractor, Morning Chores with Snow, March Rescue, Hours from Harvest, and Dowsing, *Red Dirt Roads.*

Once Upon A Time in Oklahoma

Once Upon a Time In Oklahoma

locust munched across the plains
and dust drowned the sun.

The cow leapt over the cliff
and the chicken shed her feathers.

On the seventh day
a white owl foretold flood
and the clouds burst.

We left the castle
and dried the freshest meat.
Weeds sprouted from the silt.

If we had magic beans,
golden apples,
or a princely frog,
they went into the soup pot.

Inspire Me

Sing to me, Green Muse.
Tell of fierce pilgrims
striving out of gray scarcity
toward lush pastures.

Shout of nymphs with pretty braids,
strong-armed youths
felling trees and plowing prairie.
Tell me the way they died.

Pour from wide mouth jars
myths of swaying golden fields
and sweat-scented scythes
from decades gone.

Write of stubborn women
and rogues in stiff hats,
their small wars
and deep affection.

Recall long walks and tall tales,
hoop snakes rolling tail to mouth down red hills,
poison soup, shouting preachers, and
murderous neighbors with ravenous hogs.

Whisper of banjo, canoe, and swimming hole.
Show me the floods and fires,
dreams and failures.
Sulky Muse, bring me out of the gloom

into bright light.

Those Who Came

Shoes on the Stairs
Martha Jane Rowe Myers 1844-1934

Martha Jane aligned
her shoes on the stairs,
a pair of pretty slippers,
new as the day
she unwrapped them,
on each step.
She wore instead boots
cast off by her sons.

Cherished leather in dim light,
narrowing the crude steps,
gifts her family gave her
hoarded for the hard times
she expected to return.

Those salvaged steps lead today
not up as in the old house
but down to the basement.
where her letters, molded dank,
fretful capsules

release the fumes of her life,
quaint in recollection,
fierce in living.
Her days too harsh to wear
elegant shoes at home.

Such Lies

To Martha Jane Myers, Elk Falls, Kansas
From Washington Lee Myers, Lamar, Bent County, Colorado

August 13, 1887

Dear Wife,

Now Martha, you say someone wrote you
that I was running after a bad woman.
That is a lie. There is not a bad woman here
as I have heard of. You can hear anything
if you hunt for it. I hope you will stop,
for God's sake, for me, for our children.

I don't know who it could be would write such lies about me.

You say you will now go and come when you please.
You know you always did.
You always did as you please
and there is no use to lie about that.

I don't know who it could be would write such lies about me.

You think you have found a club to kill me with,
but I thank God that club ain't heavy enough to do it.
You can hurt me, but I hope I will live all the same.
I am hurting raw and can not rest,
but you don't care or you would not have written me so.
You could give a kind word. Say you hope it isn't so.
You could be my best friend until you found out better.

I don't know who it could be would write such lies about me.

You should give up all for me,
and I should do the same,
and I will as long as I live.
We have almost lived out our lives.

I am willing to spend my days with you.
If it is a hard living, for the sake of our children, I don't care.
If you are not able to work and never sleep in my bed,
I am willing to stay with you.
Think hard and then write me a better letter.

I don't know who it could be would write such lies about me.

From your old man and true husband,
Washington Lee Myers

Traveling Man
Washington Lee Myers 1844-1911

Wash was a big man, over 200 pounds.
He made the run of '89 on a little red pony
and staked a claim
seven miles east of Norman.
Moving west and south all his life,
he trailed a string of failed schemes
and broken promises behind him.
His wife and five remaining kids
(his eldest daughter married and making her own claim)
followed him to Indian Territory,
a last chance at family life and financial security.
His oldest son died, and his youngest was born
on that claim on Fish Creek.
But fancy drink and hard women
again had more appeal than farming
so he and Martha Jane parted there.
She and her sons homesteaded further west
and he found new ears for his stories of Civil War,
freight hauling in Colorado,
building the Erie Canal,
and fishing in the Mississippi River.

For Want of Shoes
Weaver Lee Myers 1882-1959

The sun was hot,
the ax was heavy
that summer in Indian Territory.
Weaver Lee, aged seven,
split firewood with Sister Daisy
earning money for school shoes.
Their father drank that cash
and the barefoot boy stayed home.

He always said his mother,
tiny and tough lady, ferried
their goods in a wheelbarrow
the next year, in the Run of '92.
She staked an Oklahoma
Territory claim as a single woman.
Weaver worked beside her,
never went to school,
never learned to read.

She always blamed her ex's
bad behavior on the saltpeter
the Union Army fed him.

Dowsing: Weaver was a Water Witch
As told by Dale

1959.
Three years into the drought
and we needed a well.
The old man came to
witch that well.
Now I was sixteen years old
and didn't sleep
through all my science classes.
He read my doubt.
Here,
he handed me two lengths of welding rod.
Hold them out in front of you
and walk a grid across the field.
Now I had done hard work that summer,
and I had learned many harsh lessons.
But this was the stupidest thing
I'd been told to do.
Just do it, he said.
I did.
I walked back and forth across that field.
Walked until my arms ached.
Then he took the rods.
Shortly they crossed,
dipped,
pointed straight down.
Sure, I thought.
He stepped back.
The rods rose.
Now come here
and take ahold of my thumbs, he said.

Hot, tired, but thinking to humor
the old fool,
I grabbed his thumbs.
We sidestepped
back to the spot where the rods dropped,
sidestepped in some queer dance
across the field of stubble,
me hoping no one drove by to see us.
The rods shivered.
I looked to see if he was moving them
A jolt, like an electric shock,
went from his thumbs
through my body.
The water's here, he said.
Some can feel it, some can't.
He looked at me with pity in his eyes.
That well came in at 320 feet,
Rush Springs formation,
900 gallons per minute.

Irish Hired Girl
Stella Ray Myers 1896-1980

I wore a slat bonnet and long sleeves
but my skin still freckled.
I knew how to work
and how to make do.

He was courting the daughter
of that big white house.
Kin of the Texas Houstons, she was.
When she wouldn't have him,
Weaver turned to me,
the hired girl.
He played the banjo, had a row boat,
and hosted picnics on the river
by his saw mill.

I married him
and cooked for his crew
in that little house
on the quarter of land
he bought from the Cheyenne.
Had to haul water
from that river to
cook and wash.

Seems I got pregnant every
time he hung his pants on the footboard.
Lost the first two little boys.
Raised the second two.
When our first girl came,
he was so proud,
he smocked her first dress.

We struggled yet survived
through the hard times.
Fed my children
and my sisters and their families.
Life was good with a good man.

The Story Teller
Noble Chance Myers 1880-1965

He traded a shotgun for a half section
of grass at Mobeete. His brother made the
exchange to remove Chance from Custer County
after the older brother pulled a gun on a
nephew who interrupted a nap. Then one day
Chance convinced their 80-year-old
mother to climb the windmill tower while he
repaired the well.

    Chance, veteran of cattle drives,
sailor of South American seas, built
a brush corral in that Texas pasture and dug
a cave into the side of a hill to live in.

Only once did I visit Uncle Chance's
dugout, forty years after he retreated from family.
A Model T Ford sat within the corral.
He took us to the local store to show his kin

When he visited Oklahoma, Stella,
his sister-in-law, made him bathe and put on
new clothes before he came inside. He wore
a gold ring he never explained, told vivid tall
tales, smelled of wood smoke and hand-rolled tobacco.
Once when he languished in Dodge City's jail,
(he bit off an opponent's ear in a bar fight.)
his mother dreamed of his plight and went North to
bail him.
    Martha was unusual that way.

Faded
Suzie Alice Ray 1872-1957

The village held a post office
inside its only store. There was
an abandoned school, a cemetery,
and a few gray houses.
Great-grandmother's house
lacked a porch or trim
but had rocking chair,
kerosene lamp, and coal stove.

We came Saturday to split kindling for that stove.

The old woman's dress,
once blue with white flowers,
now as bleached of color
as her hair and the quilt on her bed.
I cannot recall her voice
but her hatchet I remember.

My grandmother, her daughter,
swung that sharp little ax
down on the firewood she held endwise
on the tree stump-chopping block.
With the box beside the stove filled,
we paid the bill at the stove for the older
woman's coffee and phone calls.

As we drove home, I heard about
Great-grandfather Henry Alexander Ray
who died young,
worn out by his wife's whining
and lungs destroyed by dust
in the broom factory.

Isolated Homestead
Christene Merk Fransen 1891-1962

During the time
of the Montana homestead,
she never left their claim.
Month after month,
she saw only him
and worked hard
to build a home in that cabin.
Her dad lured the young couple
back to Oklahoma with a train ticket
and the promise of a farm.

Baby Johnny slept on
in the Montana soil.

At the Trinity Ferry
Lougene Rawls Shelby 1890-1992

It was Nineteen O Four. I was fourteen years old,
a good hand with a hoe, and just months married

there in Navarro County when the letter
came to my mother from her brother.
He had lost his wife, his horse and his farm,
in that order. He needed family to come get him.

The chopping was laid by and
the cotton not yet ready to go to pickin'
and we thought that a trip would be just the thing.
So me and Luther, Brother Ben and his wife

rigged up the wagon with its boles and sheets.
As we went down the road, folks warned us
to beware of rising water up ahead.
But it was hot and dry there in Navarro County.

It was Nineteen O Four. I was fourteen years old,
tall for my age and just months married.

We thought them fellows must be jokin'.
But we found out when we reached the river.
The Trinity was full and wide, backing out into the lowlands.
We come to a slough, a little oxbow of a thing usually dry.

But it closed the road that day,
the road we had to travel to reach the ferry.
While we stopped to study how to get across,
me and my sister-in-law

17

took our jugs and walked up to the house on the hill.
In that barnyard a crew of men milled round,
fussing with some horses in the corral—
lots of horses and too many men for one farm.

It was Nineteen O Four. I was nearly fourteen years old,
could do sums in my head, and just months married.

One gap-toothed boy, no more that twelve
and sitting on a fine roan mule, smiled ugly at us
as we walked to the back door,
calling to the woman in her kitchen.

She let us fill our jugs from her pump.
We told that farmwife we was goin'
to ford that slough and catch the ferry.
Don't, she said. *The ferry wouldn't carry*

you across after dark. Stay dry on this side till morning.
We hurried back to tell the boys, our husbands.
As we studied on this, up come an old peddler,
a chicken peddler. He traded goods for chickens

along his route. *Don't listen to those silly girls*,
he told the boys. *They don't know*
what they're talking about. I've
crossed here at midnight many a time.

It was Nineteen O Four. I was fourteen years old,
dipped snuff when I had it, and was just months married.

Even not knowing if our horses would swim,
those boys listened to that peddler
rather than what we'd heard.
Nothing else would do but that we go

across that oxbow in the twilight.
That old peddler racked his chickens,
empty crates at the bottom,
chickens at the top, and drove off into the river.

Water came over his wheels, covered his lap,
reached the third layer of coops.
Those chickens got their feet wet and
squawked loud enough to summon the dead.

It was Nineteen O Four. I was nigh on fourteen years old,
good at recitation and just months married.

We followed him, swam one wagon with four horses
then the other. Our husbands felt right smart.
It was their first trip without their daddies.
We would be across the Trinity

and a ways towards Uncle's by dawn.
Now there was another fellow parked there with us
at the side of the slough and he was sick
with the jaundice, yellow skin disease, you know.

He was driving oxen and he didn't drive so good.
Well, my husband Luther and my brother Ben
used our horses and brought his wagon across.
But then there was the oxen. Yoked oxen.

It was Nineteen O Four. I was fourteen years old,
good with a rifle, and just months married.

Ben got them started, riding on one's back.
They were swimming like they knew their business
but when they reached the middle of that span,
those ox turned downstream and got astraddle

of a tree that grew there where most days it's dry.
I watched them struggle, tangled in the flood.
Well, Brother Ben was quick.
He jumped in front of those steers

and beat them in the face with his hat.
He yelled and flailed and got them turned.
They stumbled onto the shore closer to
the Trinity and the ferry and the road beyond.

It was Nineteen O Four. I was fourteen years old,
slightly far-sighted, and just months married.

We all gathered there on the landing
and yelled for the boat; the ferryman yelled back.
He would not come until tomorrow sunup.
So there we were, stranded in between

the slough and the river. The rising river.
We camped beside the flood, six wagons in all.
We didn't feel much like eating but built
a big smoky fire to keep the skeeters away,

clouds of skeeters there by the river.
We kept our mouths shut to keep from choking,
wrapped up in our blankets
and crawled under the wagons,

me and Luther under one
Brother Ben and his wife beneath the other.
I remembered my dad saying it takes a fool
to sleep in a flood plain. I didn't want to be no fool.

It was Nineteen O Four. I was fourteen years old,
able to pick 150 pounds a day, and just months married.

Too nervous to sleep, I walked down to the river
and planted a stick at the flood's edge.
Every couple of hours I'd go back and find that stick
out in the water and plant another to mark the new rise.

I was there 'bout four o'clock when dark was lessened,
swatting skeeters and worrying
at the water creeping up my stick,
when I heard a sound coming from the slough.

I saw shapes, eight of them, sneaking through the dark.
It had been twenty years since Quanah Parker's last raid.
But nothing good would come upon a camp out of the dark.
Squatting still as a stump, I watched them.

It was Nineteen O Four. I was almost fourteen years old,
tall for my age and just months married.

I picked up my marking stick and heaved it
hard as I could at the chickens sleeping in the peddler's coops.
When those birds called out scared,
the sudden ruckus waked the sleepers

and startled the creepers. All of them stood,
staring. Luther finally picked up our rifle.
I watched them thieves run back the way they came.
I think one of them was that gap-toothed boy from the corral.

Later we heard tell of travelers
drowned at camps near the Trinity,
their goods and horses disappeared.
Oh, that day was something!

It was Nineteen O Four. I was fourteen years old,
tall and strong for my age and just months married.

Genetics vs. Environment

One grandmother
had Irish skin, long legs,
slender figure.
The other was tawny,
round, and short.
Both were short tempered
and sharp tongued.
I lived with one
and look like the other.

Those Who Stayed

Chipped Marble

whirled blue on white
exposed in the newly eroded dirt
says a child lived here. That he
was indulged I guess from
the rusted hub from a tricycle wheel.

His mother wore perfume
from a clear bottle
stoppered by the nubbin
of glass laying nearby.

Dad sharpened hoes
to chop weeds
from long, hot cotton rows
and left an inch long fragment
of the file.

From deeper layers,
a crushed segment of the chained cups
that lifted water from the cistern,
springs from a buggy,
buckles from horse harness,

Only the hump of the cellar
and bricked cistern lip
remain above ground;
from the earth, shards of life
that once lived on this hill.

Surviving Species

Beyond the sagging fence,
the buzzard reigns atop
the chimney, guarding
his nest in the abandoned house.
And sagebrush crowds
the vestiges of genetically engineered grass.

Chore Clothes

Chore clothes, I said,
and the way we lived
when barn tasks were
a daily exercise returned.

Chore clothes—
not designed tough, not specially bought
but discarded daily wear,
dinner at noon,
water jugs swathed in burlap.

Snake on the rafters,
scorpion on the stove,
fleas in the bed,
kerosene in the lamps.

Smoke on the walls,
weevils in the flour,
mice in the shoes,
outhouse down the slope.

Rifle behind the door,
cocaine in the cough syrup,
frogs in the cistern,
water hauled by the tankful.

Chores that reeked
waft romantic through
nostrils clotted with years.

Section Lines

To fit a square graph
upon a round earth,
Thomas Jefferson and his surveyors
installed a correction line
to adjust to reality and
jogged the section lines
half a mile east/west
every 24 miles north/south.

As a Jewish Jubilee year
forgives all debt and sin
in fifty year cycles, and
any twenty pound weight change
requires a new wardrobe,

families could set a shelf life,
a date to reshuffle,
a correction line,
to adjust to the curve of life.

Snow, 1947

Mother, hands on hips, stood
beside the sink with its hand pump
as Dad and I stomped snow from our boots.
We had been to the picture show,
driving the truck, our only wheels.
A shoot-em-up, he said,
that Mother wouldn't like.
Years later I learned what being
forty-two weeks pregnant meant.

I won, I won. It's a girl!
I sang when Grandmother Stella told me
the baby was here. I rocked
her big red chair as fast as I could go,
my feet sticking out over the edge.
Through the living room window,
I could see snow on the cedar tree,
the one with a white-washed trunk.
She didn't tell me about ovarian tumors,
pleas for blood donors, worry about my sister.

I remember hot air from the truck heater
and the neat double tracks in the snow,
the smell of wet wool and cow manure,
Dad driving the cattle truck,
Mother shielding the bundled baby,
and me, crouping.
I didn't know kids died
from whooping cough that year.

Oh Venerable Tub!

You came into our family in 1949,
when Rural Electrification prompted
indoor plumbing. You are square,
scarred, heavy. You glitter not,
nor bubble. At times,
only our budget
kept us together.

But
stiff knees appreciate
your modest depth,
On busy days a quick and tidy splash
 meets my needs, but on the other days,
 with muscles cramped or chilly fevers,
 my body fits your narrow arms
 and your water restores me.
If you needed more gallons to reach that level,
my drought-shaped soul would cringe.
but my mass, your width, we indulge.
You were a splash pool for my babies,
a utility for a busy woman,
and now you are a comfort.
I celebrate your porcelain being,
caress the chip beside the drain.
Together we have weathered many years.

Swamp Cooler

We danced in and out of its breeze,
giggling at each cold sprinkle
striking our semi-nude bodies.
Water gurgled through
the thick, fibrous pads.
The whirling song of the central drum
reached rooms of that 1950 house
that the cool air did not.

Windmills made these arid plains
habitable for fenced cows.
Water coolers tamed
the space for humans.

July

Corn stands tiptoe,
digging claws down
to grasp water.

Dragonflies mate
in doubled flight
over the pond

and fireworks
ram into
the sky's dark womb

in a rite
of pagan excess
and danger.

My dad loved
rockets and sizzlers.
In young arrogance

I scoffed
at the penile
competition

between him
and my oldest uncle.
for the most fire power.

Only now am
I aged enough
to enjoy the burning

of wealth,
the joy of
setting a fire,

the exuberance
of explosions,
the anticipation

of lining up artillery
on the truck's flat bed,
waiting for sun to set.

The children fire
the ammunition
from a steel table

in strict order,
a falsity akin
to dressing

a heathen deity
in a sequined
g-string.

Our celebration
possible in a land
of cold battlefields.

Farm Dog's Life

Rather like a grave,
or what I think a grave smells like,
that long deep trench for new septic lines,
I hid there with the whimpering, bleeding dog.
She, a mongrel bitch, had killed the chickens.
Dad beat her.
I wept.
Now I am older than he ever was,
and I marvel at his restraint
in not shooting her.

Beetlebaum

Dad named her,
that pinto mare with foal.
When I sat atop the shed
and held out my hand,
her pink eyes rolled back in her head.

When Dad approached,
she ran at him with teeth bared.

When Uncle Harvey wrestled
a saddle onto her,
she ran backward through the fence.

Once we bought a herd of ranch cattle,
unwieldy half-brothers,
that reminded me of that horse.

Something about Fire

Two times a week,
wind at low velocity,
we gathered the house trash
and carried it to the rusty
fifty gallon barrel sitting
alone in a circle trod bare
except in April when
winter grass sprung lush.
We dumped the sacks of refuse—
old mail, empty envelopes, school papers—
into the barrel, keeping some of the
thinnest, most flammable for the top.
From our pockets came the match box,
soggy with use, with sandpaper strip
scarred and patchy. When no
grit remained, we stuck the match
on the barrel's skin. (My cool, older cousin
could ignite the match by flicking
the head off with his thumb nail.) We held
flame to thin paper and watched blazes
grow and dance. Most interesting
flames, iridescent yet timid,
came from dyes in slick advertisements.
Catalogues consigned to trash
when the new edition arrived—we ripped
into smaller, digestible parts and
fed them into the fire. Occasionally
a fiery page lifted from the barrel
and floated to be chased down and stomped.
While waiting for the fire to burn down,
we pushed a pencil-grubby homework sheet
into the ant den and lighted it to see what
the insects would do. By age eight, we knew

power, we changed trash to ash
and flirted with destruction. Often
we blistered our fingers, and sometimes
singed our bangs. We knew the horror
stories of those neighbor kids who
shirked their patrol and burned a wheat field.
And the delinquents who sneaked some matches
into the barn, destroying barn and hay.
But we responsible children
burned the trash.
Only a few of us became
intentional arsonists
or serial killers.

Sifting Ring
State Fair Swine Show

One look from the judge
and the rejected hogs walk
through the sand-floored ring,
out the far gate, back to their cages.

While the favored pigs and showmen
gather in the holding pens
waiting for another look,
another chance at the prize money,
the rejected mope back to their stalls.

On show day, pig and I,
—washed, powdered, oiled—
entered the ring.

Crab-walking beside the animal—
on the side away from the judge—
I waved for attention,
kept the animal moving
at a stately pace,

and tried to look like
a responsible owner,
one who was never
late with rations,
never went to the ball game
instead of washing the hog.

Months of investment measured
by one look from the judge,
back to the barn in shame, or
stay around for another chance.
Pigs and prize monies disappear fast
but purple ribbons stay around for years
sleeping in bureau drawers.

Too Long at the Fair

Ankle deep in foul water,
I scrubbed the show hogs.
The concrete washroom
had four faucets, one drain.

I used a pitchfork
to lift the manure from
the hay bedding around
the steers.
Between chores,
the county fair
was a gathering
of adventurous youth
with a low ratio of adults.

On the last day,
Dad loaded the animals
in the stock trailer.
But I begged two more
hours in that joyous place.
When he returned for me,
I was sitting on the iron rail
fence, the only kid left.

Now I count decades
rather than years,
and remember the feeling
of being the last to leave.

Whoa!

I pranced out
in my poufy 1960 hair
and stylish raccoon-collared coat
to see the new colt
and the gray mare attacked—
ears back, teeth bared.

Last week, I insulted
a human mother--blithely
hiring an applicant
more humble
than her child--
with the same result--
ears, teeth, charge.

My dad slowed the horse
by hitting her between the eyes
with his clenched fist.

Peculiarly Sane

He demanded
the lease in cash
not trusting oil company checks.
After buying a new truck,
a tombstone, a case of Crown Royal,
the only indulgence he could imagine
was a drawer filled with
new socks and jockey shorts.

The Gap

She pauses,
And that hesitation with a sideways glance,
signals an untold story,
a new view into a lengthy life,
one festooned with cultivated
charm, bright and unshadowed.

Yogis say the turn of direction
between inhale and exhale
is the territory where wisdom lives.
Within that gap
lie problems fought,
roads untraveled,
things edited
from her biography
of joyful confidence,
tales not fit to share
with us, her adoring audience,

the family she has
not the one she might have had.

Pioneer Woman

She lives on a frontier,
a place sparsely settled,
that land of the superannuated.
Like the pioneers who rolled out
across the prairies,
some come well prepared
by family training:
how much flour and lard to pack,
what not to carry, how to cook over a fire.
Some hire guides for details like
which trail to follow,
how many oxen to harness,
where to find game.
Others stumble forth relying on
gossip gleaned at the local market.

That vast domain of old age
has opened for settlement.
When she was a child,
few folk lived there,
a hard place
of bent and wrinkled citizens
who scattered snuff,
whittled,
and soiled their bibs.

She hopes she brought the right equipment.

Okies Then and Now

Atop a short mountain in the San Joaquin Valley,
we celebrated Uncle's ninetieth birthday.
Handed a photo for identification,
he looked past the children
to the car on which they posed.

That's a 1926 Essex. Dad bought it new.
Used it in the field. Kept jumping out of gear.
Transmission wasn't up to the work of plowing.
Traded for a '28 Dodge.
Fitted it out for camping.
Rented out the Oklahoma farm
and worked the California fruit harvest.

From another table, I heard,
They cut off our water and our peach orchard died.
Their green lawns were browning.
Told us not to worry, we would have water next year.
We platted the farm, sold it to a developer.
Moving to Saskatchewan where there's still room to farm.

What We Became

Spring Calving

Driving slowly through the
pasture, he searches for newborns
who can be mistaken for a pile
of manure in the tall grass.
Spotting one, he collects his tools
from the box on the floorboard.
Mama Cow snorts and moans
as he kneels atop her babe.
The rancher waves her off.
Grasping
one of the baby's ears--
left for female,
right for male,
he punches a yellow tag
through that tender flesh.
A squirt of iodine,
then he releases the baby.
Mother sniffs with disdain;
she needs no plastic jewelry
to identify her baby
from the 219 others
in that pasture.

Détente with Aged Bovine Females

Why is he sneaking round our pasture?
What does that fool
think he is doing,
trying to scare us girls
into that little ole pen?

Old cows must be tricked, not forced.
Park the stock trailer down the road,
out of sight, out of earshot.

Although we are ladies,
we are not softies.
However,
for some good hay, green alfalfa,
a bribe, if you will,
we may enter your silly corral.

Put some fresh feed in the bunks;
let them find it. Send in one familiar
hand, someone they know,
to close the gate.

No way, Cowboy.
You think we're young and stupid?
Just because we let you haul us to
summer grass, you think we are going to
be pushed around, crowded into a tiny
trailer? Think again, Sonny. We are
bigger than you.

Don't try to pack the chute,
They won't crowd.

You could use the electric prod
but you will never be able
to get near them again.
Might as well sell them.
Just plan on making more trips.

Bulls come and go. We stay.
We know our pastures and our people.
Live with it

At the Cattle Auction

Outside:
the bawling cattle.
Bring up Lot J 64
bellows the loudspeaker.
Thick smells of
dampened dust, cow shit, and diesel
clot the air.

Inside:
Creeks are drier than me or Dad ever saw.
I admire anyone who can farm in this drought.
OU's quarterback is playing for the other team.
It's genetic. You saying my mama's ugly?

Ads for
cedar cutting,
dead cow removal,
trucking, tires, and metal siding
line the sale ring.
Fresh manure globs
on the white retaining
wall and flecks the
metal fence rods.

Strong lights hang
below the duct work--
harsh illumination
for rapid assessments:
limps, lumps, hump backs,
twisted tails, warts, or runny eyes,

and the calf separates
from the farmer's sale lot
to the cheap jackpot where
singles sell *as is*.

In the padded theater seats,
buyers work their phones,
calculate breakevens,
then respond to the
auction chant with a nod.

The cattle,
mostly black
and black bald-faced stock,
march calmly through
the ring like beauty contestants
on a boardwalk,
pivoting calmly
as long as they
remain in the safety of
their home herd.

In the jackpot,
the round of culls,
heads rear,
ring men jump behind barriers,
and the fast parade
in one gate and out the other
becomes a rodeo.

Miscalculations

That cow looked wrong for weeks,
feeble, gaunted up. Not like
she was pregnant and ready to calve.
Well, we found her
deep in labor
and in trouble.
Reached in.
Felt a tangle of legs.
Things not right.
Hooked on the pull chain
to get that calf out
quick
before it died of trauma.
But connecting to
what felt like a hind leg,
—breech, you know,
was instead a foreleg.
Chain was on backwards.
Broke that little leg.
But got the calf out . . . and alive.
Picked him up, rushed to the vet.

But
there was another calf in there,
a hidden twin.
Dropped after we hurried to the clinic.
Died of strangulation.
Hidden he was.
That's why the tangle of hooves.
And why the mother cow looked so used up.
Saved her, and that one calf.
Sure hate it about that twin.

Morning Chores with Snow

While
wind built snowdrifts in the wheat fields
but could not wrest the flakes
away from the yellow nests
of blue stem grass, he hurried
through the new light to find
the nine heifers who had not
delivered their first calves.
After he found them,
safe and unlabored,
he scooped silage
with the tractor-loader
into the rotating bin
of the feed truck,
then augured it into concrete bunks
along the lot fence.
Eighty-four new cattle,
fresh from the sale barn
and through the working chute,
hurried to eat the steaming, sour roughage.
Then he gathered his wrench and pipe dope
to repair the hydrant the cows had rubbed,
shut off, let freeze.
On the way to the diner,
he four-wheeled through the wheat field
and counted the stockers,
any with a droopy head or snotty nose.
With all the cattle on their feet
and nosing the snow aside for green,
he checked the electric fence for deer-damage.
Standing beside the open truck door,
he removed his Carhartt coveralls and overshoes,
then reached behind the seat for a cleaner hat.

Rescue

I need help, he said.
More help than just you.
We stood at the top
of the pipe drop

looking at the calf
trapped at the bottom
of the metal-lined hole.
The calf twisted his head

to stare back. After we gathered
a rescue team, plus a John Deere
with a front-end loader,
chains and a ladder,

the cowboy climbed down, his hat
disappearing below ground level.
He fastened the chain
around the calf's neck

with the hook directly under
the bovine's throat—
off-centered, the chain
would snap the calf's neck.

The tractor lifted the loader
and the attached calf rose straight up,
neck stretched between the chain
and the weight of his body.

He landed like an
eight-hundred pound fish.
Unhooked and clear of the hole
the calf staggered on numb legs.

Sometimes we need help–
an entire crew with tools.
And the alternative
to brutality is death.

A Jumper

Working behind a series of tall, solid gates,
I moved the new cattle through the alley,
ever closer to the processing chute where,
too late to retreat, they would be vaccinated,
castrated, tagged, and deloused. As they passed
each point, I followed, swinging the silent barrier
closed behind them. Slower than a young person,
frailer too, with this system--oiled, fast, efficient--
I delivered these new calves without shouts or whips.
But this group of fifteen, separated from the larger herd
to walk in one barn door intact and out the other altered,
contained a vigorous individual who resisted the flow.
He charged at me instead of going away toward the first
gate. When I waved him away into the smaller pen, he
raced instead of being fooled by faux safety. By the third
gate, his patience was gone. From a standing start inside the
small enclosure, he jumped. Clearing the six-foot steel gate
his five hundred pound bulk sailed over my head
and he ran out the open door behind me.
Superior ability trumps engineering,
adjusting the odds between the mammals.

Art Becomes Life

Cows from Larson's
Far Side cartoons
came to my picnic.
Each time I chased them
away, they sneaked back.
They attacked the tent.
While I set it aright,
they dragged off a tarp.
They dumped the ice chest
and pushed my coat into the fire.
What tales of daring they will
tell in the feedlot.

The Faded Tractor

drags the old harrow
across the plowed field.
Its short teeth
comb the soil fine,
a seedbed flat for alfalfa.
Every careless turn,
each missed clod,
will reproach the farmer
for as many seasons
as the hay crop stands,
testifying to all passers
of his strength of focus
that autumn day
with the old tractor
and the rusty harrow.

Uneven Wear

While silver tape wraps the ragged fingers
of his leather gloves, and the palms
are black with sweat and ash,
their backs gleam pristine yellow.

Blizzard Predicted

Milk, bread, and bananas in the kitchen,
hoses disconnected,
trucks fueled,
pipes wrapped,
heifers near the barn,
hay bunks filled.
Then we wait,
wanting moisture
and fearing drifts
—rather like meditating on end-of-life trials—
knowing the forecast
and hoping
the worst misses our house.

Peak Experience

This year
wheat stubble drapes the valley
in a golden cloak,
vision of plenty and perfection.
Beautiful and eerie.

Where are the weeds? The gouges? The rust?

Once we planted
an ideal alfalfa crop,
a stand thick and uniform
enough
to support a tarp.
Mr. Cordes
stopped by the field
and told us to enjoy it
for it'd never happen twice.

We laughed

then.

Hours from Harvest

After months of pouring
borrowed dollars
into the ground,
the wheat stands
almost ripe–kernels
hardening to crack stage,
green bleached to gold.
Within hours
we may harvest
grain enough
to repay debt but
rising on the western
horizon cloud artillery
threatening to blast wheat from stalk,
then drown the survivors.

Food Stuff

Mammoth machine
rolls through the corn field
devouring plants,
spewing chopped stalks and grain
in a wide, green arch
out its spout
into the truck
trailing close behind.
Two swaths from the end--
the dessert of this field meal–
August clouds split open
and drench
machine, corn, red earth, and
trucks too heavy to pull themselves
through the mud.
Too near the finish to be deterred,
the men hitch the eighteen-wheeled semi
to the rear of the harvester
and the great beast
chews the last rows, then
tows the truck to the blacktop road.
from where it carries the load
to the trench
where corn fiber
will brew into silage.

Of Flu and Fire

Each April on a
a rare still day,
we loaded the propane tank
in the truck with shovels,
gloves, and the water tank
from the spray rig.
Starting on the leeward side
we torched the pasture.
Flames move across the field,
leaping hot and fierce, until
they reach the first burnt barrier.

We spooked the neighbor.
Cease, he said, *or else.*

Are viruses like prairie fire?
And epidemics like
the clearing of old growth?
Evolved into a clever group,
will we succumb
to the first strong, greedy species
that wants us for dinner?

Studying this awful analogy,
I know my own survival
hinges on eye glasses,
arch supports, and antihistamines.
Our pastures are greener
the years we burn.

A Plague on Them

Primal the cry of coyotes
wooing a bitch,
marking territory, or
bragging of races won.

I hope they sang last night
of geese slain
in the drought-stunted
wheat field.

Waste Nothing

Wallowing in
sloppy despair,
I remember

the feel of
baby pigs with
taut, hungry bodies,

tender hooves,
gristly muzzles.
They will eat

anything,
process
discards

turn dregs
into tasty bacon.
This nasty

depression
can be digested
into a poem

to be sliced
from my butchered
sidemeat.

Flow

Politics,
history,
and hydraulics
flow and swirl,
here pooling into fertile swamps,
there ripping savage canyons.

We grow wheat on the bottomlands
and weep in distress
when floods sweep our crop.
In the years of timely rain
we grow fat and think
we have controlled nature,
grown smart,
will live peacefully forever.

Dams erode,
systems rust,
change happens.
All we can hope for is an ax
to hack through the ceiling
letting us climb on the roof
and wait for rescue.

During the Crash

Trying to avoid
those racing around
consumed with fear
feels like moving hogs

when I learned to be
in all places
I didn't want
them to go.

To stop a charging, frightened pig,
I stood with my feet wide,
knees bent and clamped together
so the animal couldn't get his nose

into my crotch and flip me aside.

At the End of the Bull Market

In a financial crisis
investors behave like cattle.
Any surprise--
        a cat,
        a flash, or
        a flutter,
startles one calf.

He jumps against the metal feed bunk
and the clatter wakens the herd.
Each runs because the other runs
through the five-wire fence,
down the road,
over the embankment.

We found three dead,
twelve hiding under a bridge,
sixty-five grazing in new pastures,
all exhausted.

Flexed Out

No rain, drill wells.
Failed corn, plant sorghum.
No grain, make hay.
Dead pasture, go to the feedlot.

Adjust.
Balance.
Be agile.

Like the plastic molded
around Gumby's frame,
I dry out and crumble.

Unless I find a graceful pose
and a comfortable shelf,
my weakened wires will break.

Gumby and Pokey
hang out on the Antiques Road Show
and let other humanoids
manage the toy box.

My Team

In another October, I picked
my favorite football team
for their thrill factor.
Driving an open tractor,
pulling a wheat drill,
wearing ski goggles
to see through the dust,

I listened to live
Saturday broadcasts
from the radio mounted
on the green fender.
When Oklahoma State
took to the field

no win was assured,
no loss a given –
much like raising wheat.

White October
before bale modules and self-propelled harvesters

Tall trailer sways down the hill,
past the empty stop sign pole,
onto the scales. I await the buzzer,
them proceed to the flat where Pistol,
the gin man, swaddled in thick coveralls,
waves me away from the unhitched load.
He rides the tailgate until I find
an empty wagon stenciled with my name.

Brambles of ragged white tatters,
scrapes of black leaves,
exposed raised furrows, bare stalks,
piles of debris in the turn-rows. Jack
parks the harvester beside my wagon,
shifts the big hopper up and out,
dropping tons of bolls with a thud,
a shiver, and awhirl of dust. He drinks coffee,
then hammers rusty shields before
grasping overhead bars,
swinging into the seat. I can't hear
the tractor's hum
for the higher pitch of belts and brushes.

We will finish by Thanksgiving,
or Christmas,
or Valentine's Day
when no one remembers
how lush this crop grew
last summer,
green as the winter wheat
where fat red cattle graze.

The Ragweed War

was lost in the sixteenth week
when my sinus membrane surrendered.
I was overcome not by great green infection,
but dizzy nausea that broke my will.

So I pray for divine intervention,
death by frost for the fertile, fuzzy plant,
just in time for the cedar bloom.

Winter Solstice

From the bottom
now we climb.
The diving descent
a matter of form,
the ascent,
a matter of muscle–
sweaty aching muscle.
Through days bereft of light,
we push.
Between trees naked,
we march.
Under banks of snow,
we burrow,
Until we glimpse the oak leaf.
When it grows as big as
my little finger's nail,
we plant corn.

Back and Forth

Persephone, anxious to return to sun,
frets beside the dreary, smoky fireplace,
the one she so longed for last September.
She schedules fumigation of her
granary and sharpens the sickle blade.
A winter in close quarters with her mate,
trapped in domestic bliss and she limps past
rested into fury. Spring arrives and
she arises as wheat hollows its stem
and energy flows from leaf to germ site.
She stores the red table cloth and takes the
pink one from the closet. Next fall, she will
be tired and a winter dormancy with
the man who disgusts her today will sound
right and reasonable.

Purple Trees and Neon Fields

declare Oklahoma spring.

Shiny black calves nestle
into the dry grass, hidden like
Easter eggs. One male
cardinal sings atop a bare tree.
A calm day, a happy season,

while
seventy miles north,
the orgy of wind and fire
sweeps all
down to bare dirt.

One rain and a week of spring
will carpet even this ruined landscape
in new growth.
Too bad the cows that
could have converted the grass
into pounds of dollars
also died in the fire.

When I Fly

I face the curling breeze,
spread wide my strong arms
in the young dawn
and kite aloft. Below me
blood red mud tracks
through the snow.
I rise
above the heat
steaming from the silage
in its rocking basket,
above the smoke
popping from
the tractor's
exhaust.
Small black birds
scatter from the round-iced
highline. I dip one arm
and spiral higher where
a hard-eyed hawk
meets my stare.
Higher and higher
I ride the currents joyful.

Other nights
I sing in Nashville,
speak in unstudied languages,
kick a goal in the NFL,
and rescue a landing pod
crashed on the moon.

Mississippi Kite. Fallen.

Yesterday,
riding air currents,
the small hawk spiraled higher and higher,
a dark shape shrinking in the distance.

Tonight
his carcass lies like Achilles fallen at Troy.
His wide-spread wings glow
blue azure to navy.
Lifting him exposed a bloody gash
where his organs had lived.
As if on a shield, I carry
the fallen predator to the trash pile.
Three orioles circle and dive
their once and former enemy.
One lands a poop bomb on my shoulder.

March

Like whiskers on the chin
of the Winter Witch,
snow wisps across the road.
She twirls her wide skirt,
chilling us with its stirring,
swats her great broom,
and kisses, thrusting her icy tongue deeply
into our unwilling throats.
She coaxes calves from the womb
before they are read, then wraps
their tender flesh in frost. She leaches juice
from batteries, turns ponds solid, gleefully
slams our cars, twists our bones.
Hear her howling
as she dances across our lowly conceits.

Upland Eighty

That red field
abuts the poor side of town
and catches all the debris of life
on the economic edge,
plastic bags and fast food cartons,
broken toys, used rubbers.
Plowed under, plastics shatter and thin
but never go away.
Brave youngsters hike though the stunted crop
to explore railroad cars
parked on the field's northern boundary.
Beyond the tracks lay the river and catfish holes.
Fertile bottom land is in sight half mile distant,
but not a part of this dry farm
Unloved and difficult,
these acres are redeemed by
an oil well pumping steadily
at its center.

And the Wind Comes

sweeping bark off trees,
twisting roof from barn,
lifting semi-trailer trucks,
carrying away family photos.

The wind comes
baking crops,
blasting our hides,
curling cacti,
shriveling creeks to mud curls.

And the wind comes
banking snow,
blocking roads,
freezing stranded travelers,
smothering young cattle.

The wind comes
churning away top soil,
blackening the sky,
sanding eyelids,
strangling asthmatics.

Drought, blizzards, dirt storms, and tornados—
how does anything stand tall
in Oklahoma?

Oklahoma Cornucopia

As my head stills,
I hear acorns cracking beneath my feet,
and smell autumnal growth.
Breeze jangles the yellowing leaves,
and float the weakest ones
into the stream flowing gold.
A large animal coughs nearby
and a small gray bird scolds
from the Bois D'Arc tree
hung with natural green ornaments.

About the Author

Yvonne Carpenter lives on the Custer County land her great grandmother homesteaded in 1892. Farming informs her poetry and she aims to deepen her understanding of both agriculture and words. She has two books of published poetry and publications in several literary journals.

Printed in the USA
CPSIA information can be obtained
at www.ICGtesting.com
LVHW020103040224
770849LV00032B/354